LAVENDER HAZE UNDATED

JULY - JUNE
BUDGET & FINANCE PLANNER

ISBN: 978-1-959247-20-3

BUDGET & FINANCE PLANNER

BELONGS TO:

....

LAVENDER HAZE

Welcome to the Lavender Haze Budget and Finance Planner!

Congratulations on taking the first step towards achieving financial well-being and taking control of your finances. Whether you're just starting out or looking to refine your budgeting skills, this planner is here to guide you on your journey to financial empowerment. It's time to unleash your financial potential and create a solid foundation for a brighter future. Get ready to track your income, expenses, and savings with precision, set realistic goals, and make informed financial decisions. This planner is your companion and your tool for financial success.

FINANCIAL TRACKER SECTION

FINANCIAL GOAL TRACKER

ULTIMATE GOAL

ACTION STEPS

1ST QUARTER

REWARD

2ND QUARTER

REWARD

3RD QUARTER

REWARD

4TH QUARTER

REWARD

AREAS OF IMPROVEMENT

What do I need to work on to achieve my goal?

ACTION STEPS

What are my action steps?

Monthly Finance Tracker

Income Source	Amount

Fixed Expense	Expected	Actual

Savings	Amount	Balance

Groceries	Budget	Actual

Debt/Loans	Payments	Balance

Impulse Spending	Budget	Actual

Utilities	Budget	Actual

Other Expenses	Expected	Actual

	Income	Expenses	Savings	Debt
Target Amount				
Actual Amount				
Difference				

Monthly Bill Tracker

BILL	AMOUNT	DUE ON	Jan	Feb	Mar	Apr	May	Jun	Jul	Aug	Sep	Oct	Nov	Dec

Debt Payment Tracker

CREDITOR:	MINIMUM PAYMENT:
ACCOUNT #:	DUE DATE:
INTEREST RATE:	AMOUNT:

DATE	AMOUNT	BALANCE

52 Week Savings Tracker

WEEK	DEPOSIT	✓	BALANCE	WEEK	DEPOSIT	✓	BALANCE
1				29			
2				30			
3				31			
4				32			
5				33			
6				34			
7				35			
8				36			
9				37			
10				38			
11				39			
12				40			
13				41			
14				42			
15				43			
16				44			
17				43			
18				44			
19				45			
20				46			
21				47			
22				48			
23				49			
24				50			
25				51			
26				52			

Savings Goal Jar

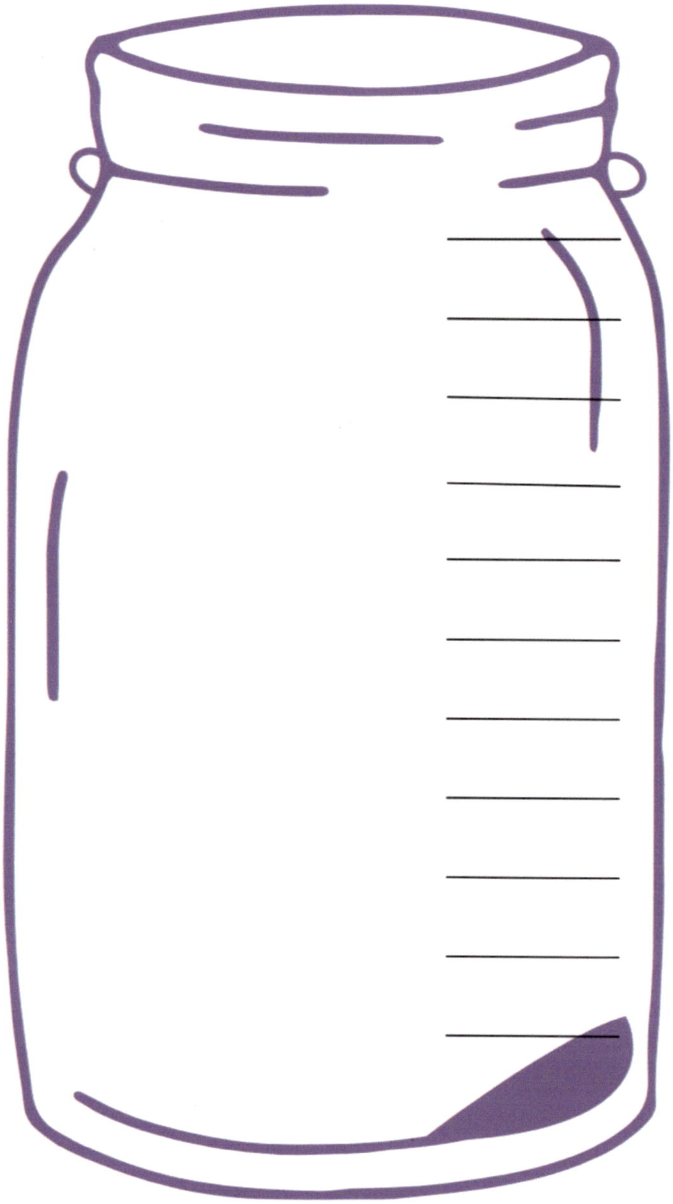

100%	$
90%	$
80%	$
70%	$
60%	$
50%	$
40%	$
30%	$
20%	$
10%	$
0%	$

Notes

Upcoming Expenses

JANUARY

FEBRUARY

MARCH

APRIL

MAY

JUNE

JULY

AUGUST

SEPTEMBER

OCTOBER

NOVEMBER

DECEMBER

HOLIDAYS

BIRTHDAYS

MISC.

NOTES.

Debt Snowball Tracker

WHAT IS THE DEBT SNOWBALL METHOD?

IF YOU HAVE DEBT ON MORE THAN ONE ACCOUNT, PAY OFF THE ACCOUNTS STARTING WITH THE SMALLEST BALANCES FIRST WHILE PAYING THE MINIMUM PAYMENT ON LARGER DEBTS.

	TYPE OF DEBT →				
DATE	Starting Balance				
Jan	Payment				
	New Balance				
Feb	Payment				
	New Balance				
Mar	Payment				
	New Balance				
Apr	Payment				
	New Balance				
May	Payment				
	New Balance				
Jun	Payment				
	New Balance				
Jul	Payment				
	New Balance				
Aug	Payment				
	New Balance				
Sept	Payment				
	New Balance				
Oct	Payment				
	New Balance				
Nov	Payment				
	New Balance				
Dec	Payment				
	New Balance				

MONTHLY PLANNING SECTION

July Finances

Income In	Amount

Fixed Expenses	Expected	Actual

Savings	Amount	Balance

Debt	Payments	Balance

Other Expenses	Expected	Actual

July Overview

	Income	Expense	Savings	Debt
Target Amount				
Actual Amount				
Difference				

Notes:

JULY GOAL/REFLECTION

GOAL

ACTION STEPS	DEADLINE

GOALS WERE MET YES NO

WHAT WORKED	WHAT DIDN'T WORK

WHAT WILL I DO DIFFERENTLY NEXT MONTH

ACTION STEPS

- [ ]
- [ ]
- [ ]
- [ ]

Notes:

August Finances

Income In	Amount

Fixed Expenses	Expected	Actual

Savings	Amount	Balance

Debt	Payments	Balance

Other Expenses	Expected	Actual

August Overview

	Income	Expense	Savings	Debt
Target Amount				
Actual Amount				
Difference				

Notes:

August Goal/Reflection

GOAL

ACTION STEPS	DEADLINE

GOALS WERE MET YES NO

WHAT WORKED	WHAT DIDN'T WORK

WHAT WILL I DO DIFFERENTLY NEXT MONTH

ACTION STEPS

- ○
- ○
- ○
- ○

Notes:

SEPTEMBER FINANCES

INCOME IN	AMOUNT

FIXED EXPENSES	EXPECTED	ACTUAL

SAVINGS	AMOUNT	BALANCE

DEBT	PAYMENTS	BALANCE

OTHER EXPENSES	EXPECTED	ACTUAL

SEPTEMBER OVERVIEW

	INCOME	EXPENSE	SAVINGS	DEBT
TARGET AMOUNT				
ACTUAL AMOUNT				
DIFFERENCE				

NOTES:

SEPTEMBER GOAL/REFLECTION

GOAL

ACTION STEPS	DEADLINE

GOALS WERE MET YES NO

WHAT WORKED	WHAT DIDN'T WORK

WHAT WILL I DO DIFFERENTLY NEXT MONTH

ACTION STEPS

- ○
- ○
- ○
- ○

Notes:

October Finances

Income In	Amount

Fixed Expenses	Expected	Actual

Savings	Amount	Balance

Debt	Payments	Balance

Other Expenses	Expected	Actual

October Overview

	Income	Expense	Savings	Debt
Target Amount				
Actual Amount				
Difference				

Notes:

October Goal/Reflection

GOAL

ACTION STEPS	DEADLINE

GOALS WERE MET   YES   NO

WHAT WORKED	WHAT DIDN'T WORK

WHAT WILL I DO DIFFERENTLY NEXT MONTH

ACTION STEPS

- ○
- ○
- ○
- ○

Notes:

November Finances

Income In	Amount

Savings	Amount	Balance

Fixed Expenses	Expected	Actual

Debt	Payments	Balance

Other Expenses	Expected	Actual

November Overview

	Income	Expense	Savings	Debt
Target Amount				
Actual Amount				
Difference				

Notes:

November Goal/Reflection

GOAL

ACTION STEPS	DEADLINE

GOALS WERE MET

YES

NO

WHAT WORKED	WHAT DIDN'T WORK

WHAT WILL I DO DIFFERENTLY NEXT MONTH

ACTION STEPS

- ○
- ○
- ○
- ○

Notes:

DECEMBER GOAL/REFLECTION

GOAL

ACTION STEPS	DEADLINE

GOALS WERE MET

YES

NO

WHAT WORKED	WHAT DIDN'T WORK

WHAT WILL I DO DIFFERENTLY NEXT MONTH

ACTION STEPS

- ○
- ○
- ○
- ○

December Finances

Income In	Amount

Fixed Expenses	Expected	Actual

Savings	Amount	Balance

Debt	Payments	Balance

Other Expenses	Expected	Actual

December Overview

	Income	Expense	Savings	Debt
Target Amount				
Actual Amount				
Difference				

Notes:

Notes:

January Finances

Income In	Amount

Fixed Expenses	Expected	Actual

Savings	Amount	Balance

Debt	Payments	Balance

Other Expenses	Expected	Actual

January Overview

	Income	Expense	Savings	Debt
Target Amount				
Actual Amount				
Difference				

Notes:

January Goal/Reflection

GOAL

ACTION STEPS	DEADLINE

GOALS WERE MET YES NO

WHAT WORKED	WHAT DIDN'T WORK

WHAT WILL I DO DIFFERENTLY NEXT MONTH

ACTION STEPS

- ○
- ○
- ○
- ○

Notes:

FEBRUARY FINANCES

Income In	AMOUNT

Fixed Expenses	EXPECTED	ACTUAL

Savings	AMOUNT	BALANCE

Debt	PAYMENTS	BALANCE

Other Expenses	EXPECTED	ACTUAL

February Overview

	INCOME	EXPENSE	SAVINGS	DEBT
Target Amount				
Actual Amount				
DIFFERENCE				

Notes:

FEBRUARY GOAL/REFLECTION

GOAL

ACTION STEPS	DEADLINE

GOALS WERE MET YES NO

WHAT WORKED	WHAT DIDN'T WORK

WHAT WILL I DO DIFFERENTLY NEXT MONTH

ACTION STEPS

- ○
- ○
- ○
- ○

Notes:

March Finances

Income In	Amount

Fixed Expenses	Expected	Actual

Savings	Amount	Balance

Debt	Payments	Balance

Other Expenses	Expected	Actual

March Overview

	Income	Expense	Savings	Debt
Target Amount				
Actual Amount				
Difference				

Notes:

March Goal/Reflection

GOAL

ACTION STEPS	DEADLINE

GOALS WERE MET YES NO

WHAT WORKED	WHAT DIDN'T WORK

WHAT WILL I DO DIFFERENTLY NEXT MONTH

ACTION STEPS

- ○
- ○
- ○
- ○

April Finances

Income In	Amount

Fixed Expenses	Expected	Actual

Savings	Amount	Balance

Debt	Payments	Balance

Other Expenses	Expected	Actual

April Overview

	Income	Expense	Savings	Debt
Target Amount				
Actual Amount				
Difference				

Notes:

APRIL GOAL/REFLECTION

GOAL

ACTION STEPS	DEADLINE

GOALS WERE MET YES NO

WHAT WORKED	WHAT DIDN'T WORK

WHAT WILL I DO DIFFERENTLY NEXT MONTH

ACTION STEPS

- ○
- ○
- ○
- ○

NOTES:

May Goal/Reflection

GOAL

ACTION STEPS	DEADLINE

GOALS WERE MET YES NO

WHAT WORKED	WHAT DIDN'T WORK

WHAT WILL I DO DIFFERENTLY NEXT MONTH

ACTION STEPS

- [ ]
- [ ]
- [ ]
- [ ]

NOTES:

June Finances

Income In	Amount

Fixed Expenses	Expected	Actual

Savings	Amount	Balance

Debt	Payments	Balance

Other Expenses	Expected	Actual

June Overview

	Income	Expense	Savings	Debt
Target Amount				
Actual Amount				
Difference				

Notes:

JUNE GOAL/REFLECTION

GOAL

ACTION STEPS	DEADLINE

GOALS WERE MET YES NO

WHAT WORKED	WHAT DIDN'T WORK

WHAT WILL I DO DIFFERENTLY NEXT MONTH

ACTION STEPS

- [ ]
- [ ]
- [ ]
- [ ]

Notes:

Notes:

Made in the USA
Monee, IL
05 November 2026

67387958R00031